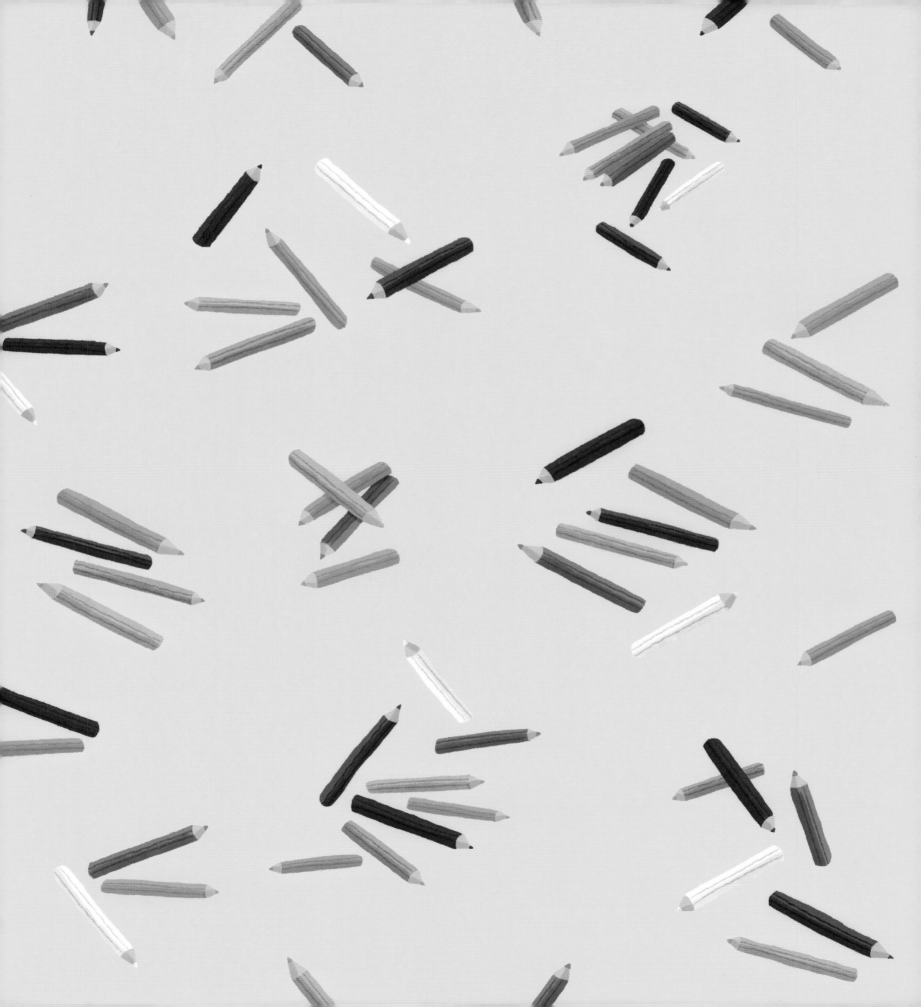

For Izzy – L.T.

For Jeni – A.A.

Published in the UK by Scholastic, 2024
1 London Bridge, London, SE1 9BG
Scholastic Ireland, 89E Lagan Road, Dublin Industrial Estate, Glasnevin, Dublin, D11 HP5F

SCHOLASTIC and associated logos are trademarks and/or
registered trademarks of Scholastic Inc.

Text © Lisa Thompson, 2024
Illustrations © Aysha Awwad, 2024

The right of Lisa Thompson and Aysha Awwad to be identified as the author and illustrator of this work
has been asserted by them under the Copyright, Designs and Patents Act 1988.

ISBN 978 0702 32453 6

A CIP catalogue record for this book is available from the British Library.

Printed and bound in Great Britain by Bell and Bain Ltd, Glasgow
Paper made from wood grown in sustainable forests and other controlled sources.

3 5 7 9 10 8 6 4

www.scholastic.co.uk

WORRY
BOOTS

Lisa Thompson

Aysha Awwad

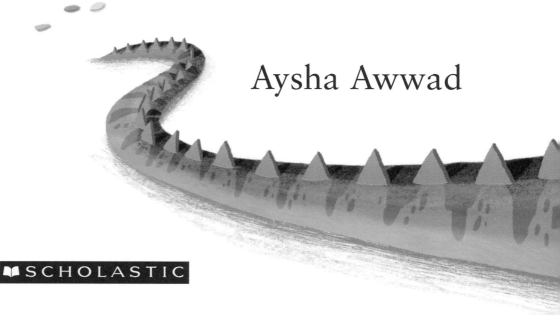

SCHOLASTIC

Connie slipped her feet into her shiny new boots.
They felt hard and awkward and very, very different.

"Let's get going, Connie," said Connie's mum.
"It's an exciting day today, your first day at school!"

But as they walked to the bus stop . . .

"WAIT, MUM!" cried Connie.
"THERE'S SOMETHING
IN MY BOOT!"

Connie wriggled her foot against the thing.
It felt lumpy and bumpy between her toes.

In fact, it felt exactly like . . .

A DINOSAUR'S BUMPY BOTTOM.
"THERE'S A DINOSAUR IN MY BOOT!"
gasped Connie.

"How dare you trample all over my bottom with your pongy foot!"

"Mum, **stop!** I **can't** go to school with a **dinosaur** in my boot! Everyone will stare at me."

Connie's tummy felt **lumpy** and **bumpy,** just like the **dinosaur's bottom.**

"Don't be silly, Connie!
No-one will stare
at you," said Mum.
"Come along.
You don't want to be late
and miss out on all
of the fun, do you?"

Connie wriggled her foot again
and the bump vanished.
"Oh," she said.
"Maybe it isn't a dinosaur after all."

"Phew!"
said the dinosaur.

Connie and her mum got on the bus.
But as they drove past the sweet shop,
Connie felt the **thing** in her boot again.

It was **hard** and **spiky**.
In fact, it felt **exactly** like . . .

A UNICORN'S HORN!
"MUM!" she yelled.
"THERE'S A UNICORN
IN MY BOOT!"

"Stop squashing
my horn with
your stinky foot!
Get off!"

"I **can't** go to school
with a **unicorn** in my boot!
Everyone will laugh at me."

Connie's tummy felt
hard and **spiky**,
just like the
unicorn's horn.

"No-one will laugh at you, Connie," said her mum as they got off of the bus. "Look! These children are going to your school, too! Maybe they'll be your **new** friends?"

Connie wriggled her foot again and the hard, spiky horn vanished. "Oh," she said. "Maybe it isn't a unicorn after all."

"Phew!" said the unicorn.

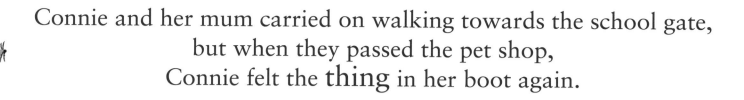

Connie and her mum carried on walking towards the school gate,
but when they passed the pet shop,
Connie felt the **thing** in her boot again.

It wasn't lumpy and bumpy or hard and spiky.
It was actually **sharp** and **pointy**.
In fact, it felt **exactly** like . . .

"I **can't** go to school
with a **shark** in my boot!
Everyone will be scared of me."

Connie's tummy felt
sharp and **pointy**,
just like the
shark's pointy tooth.

"No-one will be scared of you, Connie," said Mum. "There's your teacher over there! She looks really friendly, doesn't she?"

The teacher had a big smile on her face as she welcomed everyone into the classroom.

"Oh," said Connie. "Maybe it isn't a shark after all."

"Phew!"
said the shark.

But Connie's boot still felt a
bit funny, just like her tummy.

Connie's mum stopped at the door of the classroom
and she held out her hand.

"You won't want something in your boot on your first day of school.
Shall we get it out, Connie?" she said.

Connie wasn't so sure.
What if the thing in her boot really was . . .

Her mum tipped the boot

upside down

and out fell . . .

. . . a pebble.

bee

book

ball

cup

car

cat

"Oh!" said Connie. "Is that it?"

Connie's mum smiled. "Yes! Sometimes, when we worry about something it can feel scarier than it actually is. Like a first day at school."

Connie put her boot back on and wiggled her toes.

It felt better now.

And so did her tummy.

All the other children walked in to the classroom
and began to hang their coats on their pegs.

Welcome
Class

"Are you all right now, Connie?"
said her mum, giving her hand a squeeze.

Connie thought about it for a moment,
and then she smiled and nodded.

Maybe today **wasn't** going to be as bad as she thought . . .

. . . especially now that she had **so** many **new friends** to play with!

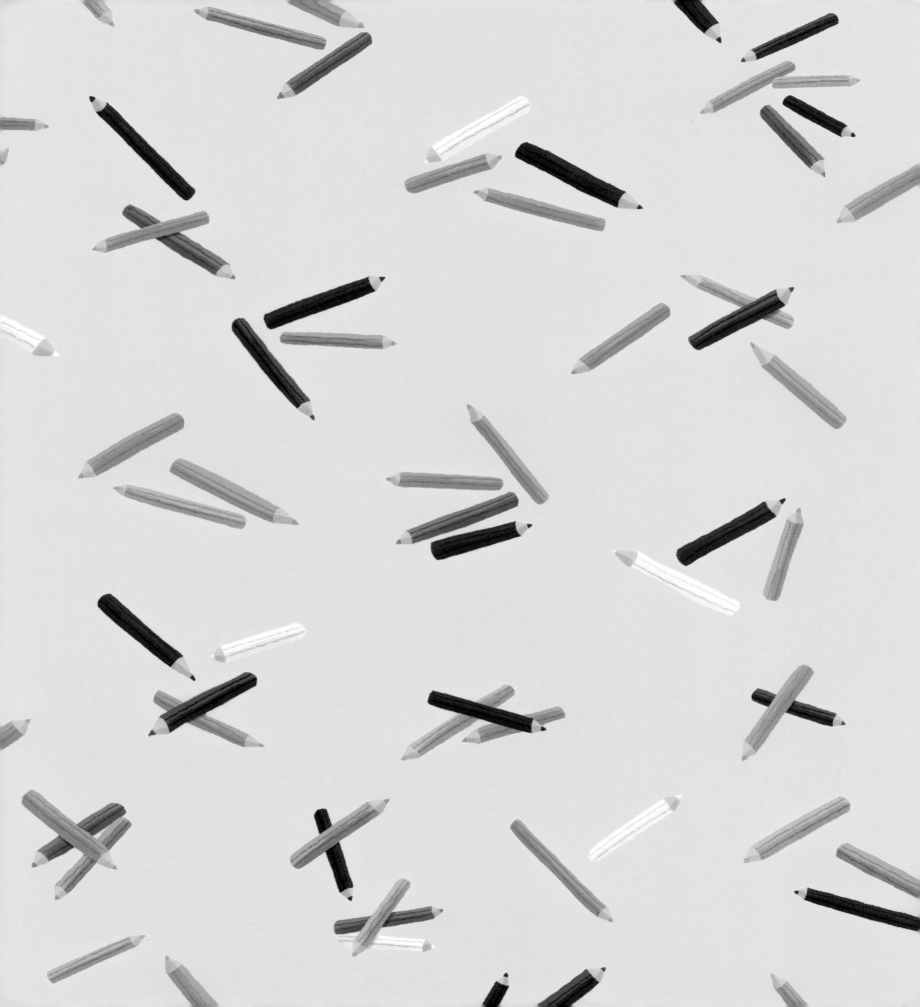

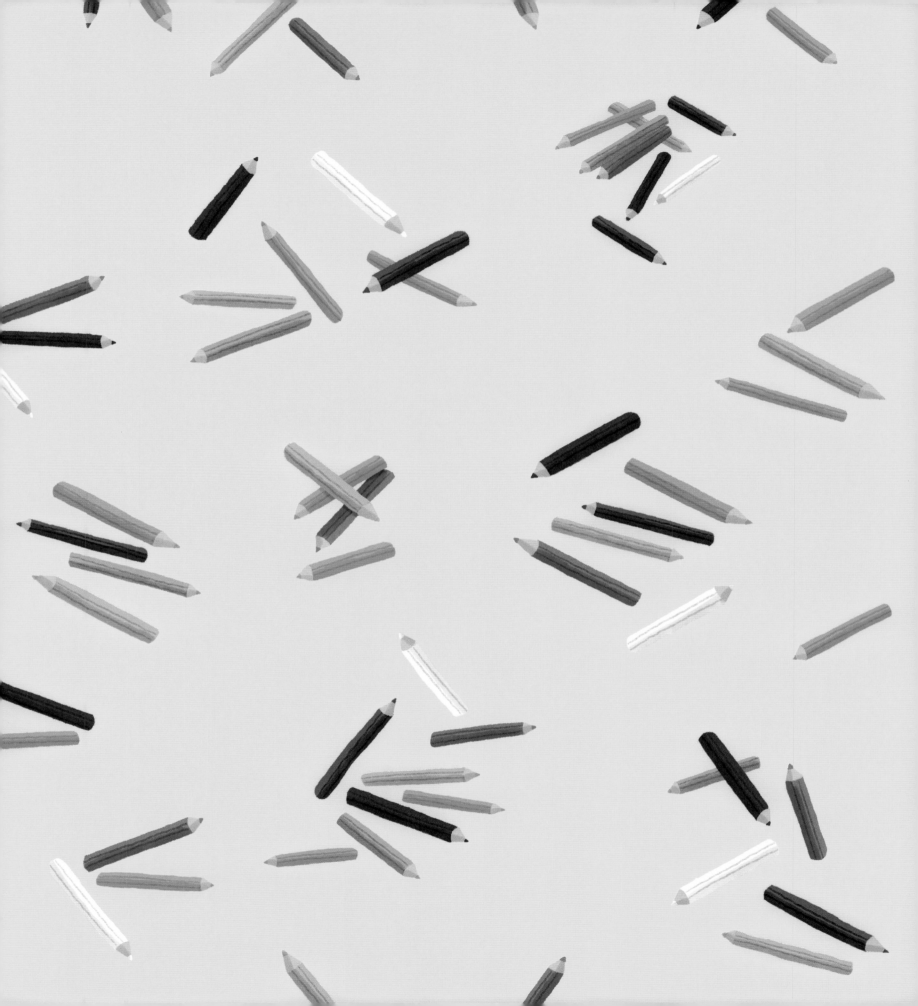